TM

MoPT

CW01430860

An Executive Guide to Portfolio Management

London: TSO

✕ TSO

information & publishing solutions

Published by TSO (The Stationery Office)
and available from:

Online
www.tsoshop.co.uk

Mail, Telephone, Fax & E-mail
TSO
PO Box 29, Norwich, NR3 1GN
Telephone orders/General enquiries:
0870 600 5522
Fax orders: 0870 600 5533
E-mail: customer.services@tso.co.uk
Textphone 0870 240 3701

TSO@Blackwell and other Accredited Agents

Customers can also order publications from:
TSO Ireland
16 Arthur Street, Belfast BT1 4GD
Tel 028 9023 8451 Fax 028 9023 5401

First published 2010

ISBN 9780113312603

Printed in the United Kingdom for The
Stationery Office

P002365186   c5   06/10

Contents

Foreword

Portfolio management is a discipline whose time has come. Recent reports from the capability reviews as well as from the National Audit Office have highlighted the importance of improved prioritization of our investment in change (projects and programmes). This is not a challenge facing the public sector alone – ensuring successful delivery and realizing the full benefits in terms of efficiency savings and contribution to strategic objectives are of relevance to all sectors of the economy and in all jurisdictions.

It is here that portfolio management plays a critical role in facilitating organizational survival and growth. By better co-ordinating our investment in projects and programmes, improving the management of risk, working together as one team and by providing accurate, timely information that enhances management decision-making, we are able to:

- Invest in the right projects and programmes in the context of the current environmental conditions, and
- Ensure successful delivery in terms of time, quality, budget and benefits realization.

This guide has been prepared to provide senior executives with an overview of portfolio management – the principles upon which it is based, some of the techniques used, and how you can get started and sustain progress. I commend it to you.

Nigel Smith
Chief Executive, Office of Government Commerce

Acknowledgements

The Office of Government Commerce (OGC) acknowledges with thanks the contributions of Craig Kilford and Stephen Jenner in the creation of this executive guide. In addition, OGC would like to thank the following people in recognition of their contribution in reviewing the guide.

Tim Banfield	National Audit Office
Nicky Bloomer	ACPO (TAM)
Tracey Collingwood	Head of Centre of Excellence, Highways Agency
Martin Crumpton	Head of PPM Centre of Excellence, Department for Transport
Tim Ellis	Head of Programme Office, Royal Borough of Kensington and Chelsea
Helen Goulding	Ofgem
Peter Hartley	KPMG
Paul Hirst	DTPO, HM Revenue and Customs
David Palmer	Home Office
Michael Pears	Department for Children, Schools and Families
Paul Rayner	Logica plc and ProgM, the programme and portfolio management specific interest group
Stephen Tatler	HM Revenue and Customs (PPM centre)
Sue Vowler	Project Angels Ltd
David Watkinson	Identity and Passport Service
Andy Woodward	Department of Health Informatics Directorate

Introduction

This guide is about portfolio management and is specifically aimed at senior executives – the subject is discussed from a strategic perspective so much of the detail will be included in the forthcoming practitioner guidance (see www.best-management-practice.com for latest information). Furthermore, we have tried to remove as many technical terms and abbreviations as possible; however, a few must remain to ensure that everyone speaks the same language (a glossary is included).

This guide has been written specifically to help you better understand how portfolio management can assist in addressing the challenges you and your organization are facing – challenges on the one hand posed by tighter fiscal conditions and the need to deliver greater value for money, and on the other, the need to respond to demands for more customer-focused and effective services.

Whilst the guidance is non-sector-specific, a particular focus is given to the role it plays in helping the public sector adapt to these challenges.

This guide answers the following questions in turn:

1   What is portfolio management – what is it designed to achieve and how?

2   How does portfolio management fit into the bigger organizational picture?

3   What will I get from it – and how can the potential benefits be realized?

4   How can we get started and how do we sustain progress?

5   What are the key questions I should be asking?

Conditions in 2010 mean that the case for portfolio management is even more compelling than when conditions were more economically favourable. This is because it enables organizations to achieve more from less by:

- Providing information that enables the 'right' investment decisions to be made
- Monitoring the composition of the portfolio to ensure it remains strategically aligned and that performance stays on track
- Managing the allocation of resources to deliver chosen projects and programmes more cost-efficiently
- Promptly reallocating resources where activities no longer represent the optimum allocation of scarce resources
- Actually realizing benefits promptly in terms of efficiency savings (by redeploying staff time saved, for example) or achieving a quantifiable contribution to a strategic objective or business priority.

Real-life experience

A survey[1] of 125 medium to large-size companies from the UK, Europe and the rest of the world by researchers from London and Ashridge business schools in 2005 found a strong correlation between increasing adoption of project portfolio management processes and a reduction in project-related problems, as well as improved project performance, and this link increased with the maturity of the processes adopted.

1 What is portfolio management?

To be successful, organizations must evolve and this means improving how they run their business on a daily basis (business as usual) and adapting to emerging demands and expectations. Portfolio management helps organizations make decisions about implementing the right changes to business as usual; those changes are delivered via projects and programmes. It also provides a 'helicopter view' of all change activities – both those in planning and those in delivery – including providing a clear line of sight about what is in the portfolio, what it is costing, what risks are faced, what progress is being made, and with what impact on business as usual and the organization's strategic objectives.

Rather than representing a new discipline, portfolio management seeks to build on, and better co-ordinate, existing processes such as strategic planning, investment appraisal and project and programme management. Portfolio management is not concerned with the detailed management of these projects and programmes; rather, it approaches the management of change projects and programmes from a strategic viewpoint, focusing on the key issues outlined above. This is reflected in the following formal definition for portfolio management, which is:

> a co-ordinated collection of strategic processes and decisions that together enable the most effective balance of organizational change and business as usual.[2]

Portfolio management can be used effectively within specific directorates of the organization – for example, the 'IT portfolio'. However, the greatest success is realized when management boards use portfolio management to deliver the organization's corporate change portfolio as a whole. To enable the concepts to be more readily expressed and understood, we focus on the change portfolio for the rest of this guide.

Portfolio management addresses the fundamental questions:

- Are we doing the right things?
  - Are we confident that we are allocating our resources to those change initiatives that contribute most to our strategic objectives, even when funding and short-term priorities change?
  - Is our investment in change achievable and are we taking into account the organization's limited resources and capacity to change?

Real-life experience

The National Audit Office reports that good portfolio management at board level helps ensure that decisions about the priority of programmes and projects are clearly in line with the organization's business strategy, that there is the capacity to support them, and that the portfolio represents the optimum balance between benefits and risk.[3]

- Are we doing these things right?
  - Does 'performance match the promise'? Are our changes being delivered on time, to specification and to budget? Is project and programme delivery being achieved as cost-efficiently as possible? Are we managing interdependencies effectively?
- Most significantly, are we realizing all the **benefits** in terms of more effective services and efficiency savings from the changes we are implementing? This goes beyond tracking against the forecasts used to justify investments to ensuring that unplanned benefits are identified and lessons learned are disseminated and acted upon.

Real-life experience

The portfolio management approach applied to managing the Criminal Justice System's IT portfolio (which included projects in the Home Office, Ministry of Justice and Crown Prosecution Service) was credited with increasing benefits threefold and won the 2007 Civil Service Financial Management award.

The mechanisms by which these questions are answered are incorporated in the model shown in Figure 1.1. This model brings together the key activities required to successfully define and deliver a portfolio of change whilst ensuring resources are used efficiently.

Figure 1.1 The portfolio management cycles

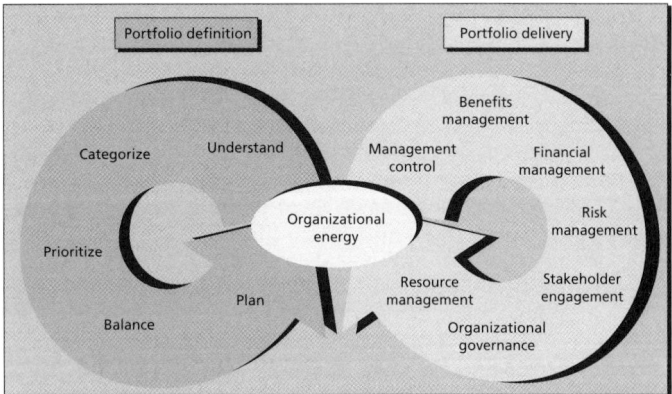

A key point to note is that the two cycles are driven by 'organizational energy'. This highlights that effective portfolio management is more than a series of processes – success can only truly be realized if the collective efforts of the people working for the organization are focused on the appropriate goals and they have a sense of working together as one team. In the context of portfolio management, organizational energy includes elements such as senior management commitment and communication; a mutual and shared desire to succeed based on effective employee engagement; effective governance and leadership; and culture and behaviours reflective of a focus on the overall good rather than individual or silo-based interests. 'Groupthink'[4] is, however, an ever-present danger – senior managers should therefore promote an environment of constructive challenge and independent scrutiny.

There are six key points to note at this stage:

1 **Portfolio management can be applied at the organization, directorate or functional level** However, this guide concentrates on the application of portfolio management to an organization's total investment in business change (i.e. the projects and programmes that are designed to improve business as usual) and not the cost of business as usual

2 **There is no 'one size fits all' approach** Experience and academic and industry research has confirmed that the key principles described in this guide need to be adhered to, but their specific application needs to be tailored to the organizational circumstances. Each organization is unique and so portfolio management should be modified to suit the strategic objectives, business priorities, existing processes, governance and funding availability, as well as the environment in which the business operates

3   **Portfolio management is about managing the organization's portfolio definition and delivery processes in a more integrated and disciplined way** That's not to say that you should follow rules blindly, but that variations should be as a result of a deliberate management decision

4   **Portfolio management is about ensuring appropriate and reliable evidence is provided to inform executive decision-making** For example, decisions about the allocation of limited resources must be based on evidence rather than applying a process-based 'strait jacket' or constraint to exercising management discretion. The focus is also on ensuring that the basis of such decisions is clearly understood so that there is clarity about why projects are undertaken, what they will cost, and what benefits will be realized in terms of cashable savings or some quantified contribution to strategic objectives

5   **It's about having a 'clear line of sight' from strategic intent to benefits realization** This is in preference to swamping senior managers with reams of reports on project and programme progress. A key benefit of portfolio management should be more rapid, flexible and consistent decision-making as investment criteria and the format of proposals are standardized and streamlined

6   **Portfolio management should pay its way** You do not necessarily need new software systems, as these work for some organizations but not all. Ideally a portfolio office will consist of people with the right skills in portfolio management. In addition, many organizations ensure other departments work collaboratively, sharing skills in project and programme management, finance, business planning, management information etc. Any additional expense should be more than

offset by savings from more consistent and streamlined processes, more rapid decision-making, and the removal of low-value, duplicate and poorly performing projects.

What arises from this is the central importance of prioritizing the allocation of scarce funds in terms of:

- **Return or attractiveness** This should be in terms of the forecast contribution to business objectives, whether that contribution concerns new or improved services or achieving cost efficiencies
- **Risk or achievability** This encompasses consideration of both successful delivery of the project and realization of the forecast benefits.

This is not a one-off exercise, but a dynamic, iterative process designed to ensure continued prioritization, strategic alignment and balance in the context of a constantly changing environment.

2 How will portfolio management integrate with my organization's current processes?

The successful implementation of portfolio management depends on how well it is integrated with existing organizational processes. This includes the relationship with business as usual; strategic/business planning and investment appraisal; budgeting and resource allocation; project and programme management; performance management; and corporate governance.

2.1 PORTFOLIO MANAGEMENT AND BUSINESS AS USUAL

The relationship between portfolio management and business as usual is a discussion that takes place in most organizations when implementing portfolio management. This relationship is illustrated in Figure 2.1 as a simple concept – 'Run the business, change the business' – showing how they combine to achieve strategic objectives. In short, portfolio management controls the changes to business as usual; when changes are successfully implemented, business as usual improves and benefits are then realized. It is this balanced, cyclical relationship between portfolio management and business as usual that helps achieve strategic objectives.

Figure 2.1 Portfolio management and business as usual

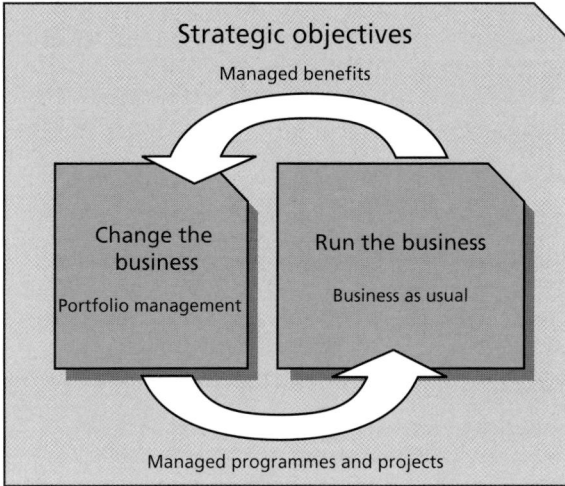

2.2 STRATEGIC/BUSINESS PLANNING AND INVESTMENT APPRAISAL

Portfolio management does not seek to repeat or replace strategic and business planning; rather it seeks to ensure that the organization's projects and programmes represent the optimum allocation of finite resources in the context of changing circumstances. Strategic planning therefore sets the context within which portfolio management operates by providing:

■ The basis for determining the scope of the portfolio of projects and programmes and the basis on which prioritization decisions can be made. As part of strategic planning, portfolio management addresses two fundamental questions:

- Are the projects and programmes in our portfolio the 'right ones' in the context of our strategic objectives?
- Is our portfolio, together with business-as-usual activities, sufficient to achieve our strategic objectives?

■ The success measure against which portfolio performance will ultimately be assessed is whether or not the changes to the business have helped your organization achieve its strategic objectives.

Real-life experience

The *Harvard Business Review* has reported that SmithKline Beecham increased the expected value of its drug development portfolio by around $2.6bn (25%) without any corresponding increase in spend via more rigorous prioritization and allocation of available spend.[5]

This relationship between strategic planning and portfolio management is two-way – the former provides the context within which the latter operates. However, portfolio management provides information on the contribution that projects and programmes are providing to the strategic objectives.

2.3 BUDGETING AND RESOURCE ALLOCATION

Strategy is made real at the point at which resources are deployed. Portfolio management provides the means by which the link between strategy and resource allocation can be maintained.

Budgeting is often a key challenge because every organization does it differently. Some have devolved budgets with directors controlling the budget for all business as usual and projects and programmes within their directorate. Others, with higher levels of portfolio management capability, have adopted an approach where the project and programme budget is owned jointly by the management board with funds only being allocated to projects and programmes at the point of an agreed business case – and these allocations are subject to ongoing assessments of viability and approval by the board as a whole. This can be an extremely powerful approach; however, it can be challenging to establish given perceptions of its impact on individual autonomy. Where such fears can be overcome, the benefits are potentially huge from more effective joint working in pursuit of shared corporate goals.

Real-life experience

Jeffery and Leliveld[6] at Massachusetts Institute of Technology (MIT) reported that those who reach what they term a 'synchronized' level of portfolio management achieved cost savings of 40%. Weill and Ross[7] reported that an MIT study of more than 300 enterprises in 23 countries found growth and agility were linked to a portfolio approach.

2.4 PROJECT AND PROGRAMME MANAGEMENT

Whilst project and programme management are about managing projects and programmes at the individual level, portfolio management extends this to the corporate level and the active management of limited resources such as skilled project managers, overall risk, and dependency management. What this also means is that project scheduling may be sub-optimal at the project level, but optimal at the portfolio level; i.e. a project may well be slowed to benefit the portfolio as a whole.

2.5 PERFORMANCE MANAGEMENT

Portfolio management is more than monitoring project and programme progress at the individual level. It also requires that we monitor progress at the portfolio level, reporting whether we are delivering as planned; whether resources and interdependencies are being effectively managed; and whether benefits are being realized. This is usually achieved via a regular dashboard report which must link the portfolio plans clearly to performance. Tough decisions may need to be made as a result; a recent NAO report[8] noted that according to non-executive directors, whilst senior management in departments increasingly have access to the necessary information to reallocate resources, too often the difficult decision is not made. On the other hand, effective portfolio management also provides the data to enable action to be taken to address delivery issues on poorly performing but strategically necessary projects and programmes. The key questions are: does the report provide a clear line of sight from planning to performance, and is it used on an active basis to drive improved performance?

2.6 CORPORATE GOVERNANCE

Portfolio management supports good governance because it links delivery of the organization's strategic objectives with investment in change. Good portfolio management clarifies the responsibility and accountability for making decisions on which projects and programmes will be funded and on what basis.

3 What will I get from it?

So far we have talked about what portfolio management is designed to achieve and how it aligns with existing organizational activities. This section is about you as a senior executive, and the value you should see when portfolio management is adopted in your organization. Some of the key things you will notice include:

- Faster, more consistent and more transparent decision-making. You will have a clearer view of what projects and programmes are planned and under way, what they will cost, how they are progressing and what benefits will be realized
- More of the right projects and programmes are undertaken, and earlier removal of any that do not align to strategic objectives or that are performing poorly
- A balanced portfolio in terms of risk, timing and overall contribution to strategic objectives
- More efficient use of limited resources, including money, staff and management attention
- Greater transparency and accountability
- More reliable business delivery via improved management of:
  - the project/programme pipeline – to ensure that the flow of new projects and programmes reflects organizational capacity and resource availability
  - interdependencies between projects and programmes for the overall benefit of the organization – even if that means rescheduling some
  - organizational constraints including skills, resources and the capacity to absorb and cope with change
- More effective performance management – redirecting resources to priority activities or away from projects that do not deliver or are no longer a priority

■ Increased benefits realization via active management to ensure that the business actually changes and to exploit the capabilities delivered to them.

These benefits will grow as the organization incorporates portfolio management into its daily business routine. Investment now will enable both quick wins and future dividends. In a report for the Cabinet Office in 2008, significant benefits were reported from achieving basic levels of portfolio management. Just establishing an organization-wide view of all active and planned projects can provide substantial financial savings by providing the opportunity to remove low-value, duplicate or poorly performing projects, and by gaining an insight into how investments in one part of the organization can be exploited elsewhere. These benefits are not, however, automatic – realizing the benefits of portfolio management needs belief and effort from the very top of the organization, particularly in the following areas:

■ **Proactive and visible senior management commitment and communication** This is identified again and again as being absolutely crucial to effective portfolio management

■ **Skilled people** Executive management needs to make decisions and therefore a function must exist to provide timely and accurate information to facilitate that decision-making process. The ideal scenario is often the existence of a portfolio office. This can take various forms dependent on your organizational circumstances (more information on this is provided in the *Portfolio, Programme and Project Offices* (P3O®) guidance[9]). For example, it could be a physical team of people (this is usually the case in most large organizations), or it could be a virtual team or an amalgamation of existing functions. The critical points are that the portfolio office reports into the top of the organization and it needs to be sufficiently independent and skilled to ensure that the analyses produced are credible, reliable and timely

- **An incremental or staged approach to development of portfolio management** This approach should focus on areas of greatest need, building confidence via 'quick wins'
- **Flexible resource allocation** Such flexibility will enable the portfolio to adapt to changed circumstances with minimal wasted investment. This requires staged release of funds as confidence grows, and the use of a standard lifecycle for project and programme delivery. The lifecycle will ensure that reviews take place to confirm the continued viability of projects and programmes
- **Performance management** The old management adage 'what gets measured gets done' tends to be true. So measuring portfolio performance (in terms of spend against budget, delivery and benefits realization) sends a clear message about what senior management values
- **Assessing progress in implementing portfolio management** Progress should be assessed on a regular basis to determine whether the anticipated benefits are being realized and if not, what action is required. This in turn requires that you set clear success criteria at the planning stage, just as you would with any change programme.

It is also helpful to learn from others – issues are rarely unique and someone somewhere has probably had to grapple with the issues you are facing today. The accompanying practitioner guidance provides a source of helpful information on various approaches to common issues, as does the growing literature in this area.

Where this can be achieved the benefits are significant – in addition to those listed earlier, the organization will benefit from reduced waste, more reliable delivery and improved contribution to strategic objectives – and moreover, the ability to demonstrate this.

4 How do we get started and sustain progress?

The best way to introduce portfolio management is to take a staged approach, focusing on areas of greatest need, and building on current organizational processes and governance arrangements. There are two key elements to consider, namely defining the portfolio and then delivering it. These are described in more detail below.

4.1 PORTFOLIO DEFINITION

- **Understand** Make sure you understand the strategic objectives the portfolio is trying to achieve, the success criteria associated with these strategic objectives and hence, the scope of the portfolio and the measures to which it should contribute
- **Categorize** Organize the changes within the portfolio into groupings or segments that clearly indicate how the changes align and contribute to the strategic objectives. Such 'segmentation' also enables investments to be compared on a level playing field
- **Prioritize** Cost–benefit appraisal is the recommended approach to investment (and is recommended in HM Treasury's *Green Book*[10]). Nevertheless, it is also recognized that cost and benefit estimates are often very unreliable and that particularly in the public sector, factors other than financial return on investment need to be taken into account in investment appraisal and portfolio prioritization decisions. For this reason, it is recommended that multi-criteria analysis, including such factors as strategic contribution and risk or achievability, are considered alongside financial return on investment or net present value

- **Balance** Once projects have been prioritized, undertake a review to ensure that the proposed allocation of resources reflects organizational priorities and that there is an appropriate balance between the various strategic objectives, short- and long-term investments, direct return and capacity-enhancing investments, and low-risk/low-return and higher-risk/higher-return projects
- **Plan** Once projects have been prioritized and the portfolio balanced, the final step is to draw up a portfolio delivery strategy, including a top-level overview of the portfolio and how it will deliver the strategic objectives; the key milestones against which progress will be monitored; a cost profile; a plan for when benefits will be realized; and key risks and dependencies. This will also include a final sense check that the portfolio is achievable given available resources and that projects and programmes are appropriately sequenced.

Real-life experience

Her Majesty's Revenue and Customs (HMRC), faced with a significant funding reduction, used information on cost, delivery confidence and benefits realization to recommend prioritization options to the executive committee, who wanted to do fewer things but do them well.

4.2   PORTFOLIO DELIVERY

- **Management control** This includes:
    - Defining and communicating the portfolio management processes
    - Regular progress reporting in the form of a dashboard report – covering progress against budget, milestones, benefits and risks. The dashboard report should be the ultimate version of the truth with regards to status

- Drawing up a consistent set of templates and guidance to streamline the production of business cases and other submissions
- Periodic programme- and project-level gate or stage reviews and portfolio-level reviews

Detailed guidance on establishing effective management controls is available in the *Portfolio, Programme and Project Offices* (P3O) guidance.[9]

■ **Benefits management** At the portfolio level, this includes:
- establishing consistent approaches to the classification and valuation of benefits in business cases
- consideration of benefits at project stage/phase gates and portfolio-level reviews
- consideration of benefits in the regular portfolio dashboard reporting.

As stressed earlier, this should be an active process going beyond tracking against forecast to consider how capabilities can be exploited, lessons learned, and unplanned benefits disseminated. As such a portfolio approach to benefits management helps address the common problem of how to ensure sufficient focus is maintained after a project or programme closes. For example, projects often claim to save part of a person's time – at the portfolio level, someone should be asking how all these 'part of a person' savings can be combined to save money or increase value. A portfolio view of benefits can also help identify examples of double counting

■ **Financial management** Spend against budget needs to be monitored throughout the year, both at the individual project or programme and at the portfolio levels, to ensure planned delivery remains affordable. Again, an overview of this should be included in the regular portfolio dashboard report

- **Risk management** At the portfolio level, risk management is very different from risk management at the programme and project level. Here you are concerned with strategic risks such as overdependence on a single supplier; the availability of limited resources (skilled staff, for example); the impact of external market or economic factors; the impact of interdependencies on delivery; and flexibility in resource allocation – if conditions change, can you reallocate funding without incurring substantial wasted expenditure? This again requires that risks, and the effectiveness of any mitigating action, be included in the regular portfolio reporting

- **Stakeholder engagement** A consistent approach to stakeholder communications should be applied across the portfolio – this is another area where improved co-ordination can deliver significant efficiency savings. It is critically important to remember that stakeholder engagement is a two-way process and not just pushing information out to an audience. Feedback is essential

- **Organizational governance** Portfolio management decision-making should be aligned with the organization's governance structure. This usually means that decisions about inclusion in the portfolio and responsibility for oversight of portfolio progress lie with a business change board and/or investment committee. This board/committee needs to be supported by a virtual or actual portfolio management function charged with establishing and operating the management and other processes identified above

- **Resource management** This concerns the management of the impact of approved programmes and projects on available skills, facilities and equipment to ensure demand and supply are matched. The portfolio office needs to have sufficient details of demand (from projects and programmes) and supply, both within the organization and those that may be contracted into the organization.

4.3 ORGANIZATIONAL ENERGY

Figure 1.1 shows that the twin cycles of portfolio definition and delivery are powered by 'organizational energy'. This incorporates a range of elements that are fundamentally about people and how their efforts can be mobilized in pursuit of the organization's goals. It is very easy to put a new business process in place, but if people are not motivated appropriately, no new way of working will be adopted effectively. The key elements of organizational energy include culture, behaviour, motivation and leadership. The following actions can help to create such an environment; however, it is important to note that these are just examples. Only you have the insight to know what will work in your organization.

- Developing a shared, inclusive and engaging vision of the future and the role of portfolio management in achieving this
- Visible team work and collaborative decision-making at board level with key messages of team work being communicated to the organization from the highest level
- Aligning the organization's incentives, rewards and recognition processes with the behaviours that support a portfolio-based approach
- Use of creative new media to help communicate key messages in a more personable way. Examples of people learning from others are provided by the use of social media platforms such as Twitter and YouTube and embedding integrated audio into the standard project and programme management framework
- Engaging and listening to people so that ideas are heard and adopted where relevant
- Creating an environment where people can excel and where needless bureaucracy is recognized and removed
- Promoting a flexible working environment wherever possible to help accommodate people's personal life situations.

Real-life experience

At American Express the application of portfolio management was credited with helping to break down silos and providing an objective means to allocate and reallocate resources in a depoliticized manner. The contribution to the organization's strategic success was recognized by American Express winning a number of prizes and being cited by Wall Street analysts as enabling resource allocation flexibility.[11]

4.4   HOW DO WE SUSTAIN PROGRESS?

Sustaining progress can be a real issue. After an encouraging start, many implementations rapidly run into difficulties – notwithstanding investments in staff, training and new software, the whole process can become bogged down in internal politics, silo-based interests and inertia. The lessons learned from those that have avoided or overcome these issues, are that continued progress is assisted by:

- A senior-level sponsor to maintain focus at the highest level and to continually promote a portfolio-level view
- An incremental or staged approach, starting with areas of greatest need to demonstrate the value of portfolio management with some 'quick wins'
- Building on existing organizational processes and not reinventing wheels or changing things that do not need changing
- Managing implementation as a change programme with a business case, planned delivery, and clear success criteria
- Regular assessment of progress – not just in terms of meeting milestones but also in relation to the benefits realized. Assessments using the OGC's P3M3® maturity model can be a valuable tool here

- Adopting the 'champion-challenger' model where processes are open to challenge and improvement – but until successfully challenged, all agree to adhere to the 'champion' process
- Appropriate use of software tools tailored to support organizational needs.

5   Key questions I should be asking

We close with a series of questions that we encourage senior managers to ask of themselves and their organizations. This is presented in a format that can aid the preparation of an action plan to guide the adoption of more effective portfolio management. You might like to use this as your own personal health check for portfolio management. At the very least, we would encourage you to ask your portfolio manager to explain how any questions with a 'no' or 'partly' answer will be addressed to your satisfaction.

Key question		Yes	No	Partly	Action required
1	Do I have a clear view of the current corporate change portfolio?				
	a What projects and programmes are included?				
	b What are the predicted costs and benefits at a portfolio level?				
	c Are the interdependencies visible to me and are we managing them effectively?				
	d How will this change portfolio impact on the business?				

Key question			Yes	No	Partly	Action required
2		Given our strategic objectives, are all programmes and projects included in the portfolio necessary? And is it clear:				
	a	How each project or programme contributes to our strategic objectives?				
	b	That all funded projects and programmes contribute more than they cost?				
	c	That the selected solutions are being achieved cost-effectively?				
3		When the portfolio and business as usual are looked at together, am I confident that these are the investments that will achieve the organization's strategic objectives?				
4		Are people happy, motivated and driven to successfully implement changes to the organization?				
	a	Do people understand where we are going?				
	b	Do people understand the importance of their role in the journey?				
	c	Do people crave success and work as one portfolio delivery team?				

	Key question		Yes	No	Partly	Action required
5	Do I have a clear view of the future change portfolio, including projects in the development pipeline?					
	a	Is the start-up of projects disciplined; i.e. are effective controls in place so that significant resources are only committed to priority projects?				
	b	Are projects progressing through the development pipeline at an acceptable speed?				
6	Project prioritization – do we have a consistent set of metrics for assessing the attractiveness (return) and achievability (risk) of potential investments?					
	a	Do we make collective decisions about the projects and programmes to be included in the portfolio, or is it a situation of 'he/she who shouts loudest'?				
7	In terms of financial management:					
	a	Is the allocation of funds staged and linked to project performance?				
	b	Is a modular approach to project development in place, so that wasted spend is minimized if funding is reallocated?				
8	Are resource demand and supply matched – do we have the right people at the right time with the skills to deliver the portfolio?					

Key question			Yes	No	Partly	Action required
9		Do regular portfolio progress reports provide a clear line of sight on portfolio delivery and impact?				
	a	Do I feel confident that the reported status reflects real status?				
	b	Do I have a clear understanding of the top risks and issues facing the portfolio?				
	c	Are portfolio progress reports the basis for action rather than a template-filling exercise?				
10		Is the return and risk of individual projects actively managed – to increase the former and reduce or mitigate the latter?				
11		Do I clearly understand the portfolio management governance process?				
12		Do I have a clear view of our track record in terms of delivering projects:				
	a	On time?				
	b	To budget?				
	c	To quality?				
	d	With forecast benefits actually being realized in practice?				
13		Am I clear about the difference portfolio management has already made and will make to my organization?				

References

See www.ogc.gov.uk for the latest developments on portfolio management.

1   Reyck, B. D., Grushka-Cockayne, Y. D., Lockett, M., Calderini, S. R., Moura, M. and Sloper, A. (2005). The impact of project portfolio management on information technology projects. *International Journal of Project Management* 23, pp. 524–537.

2   Definition as agreed by OGC and Cabinet Office for the original public consultation draft of this guidance.

3   National Audit Office (2006). *Delivering Successful IT-enabled Business Change.*

4   Janis, I. (1972). *Victims of Groupthink.* Houghton-Mifflin, Boston.

5   Sharpe, P. and Keelin, T. (1998). How SmithKline Beecham makes better resource-allocation decisions. *Harvard Business Review*, March–April 1998.

6   Jeffery, M. and Leliveld, I. (2004). Best practices in IT portfolio management. *MIT Sloan Management Review*, Vol. 45, No. 3.

7   Weill, P. and Ross, J. (2004). *IT Governance: How Top Performers Manage IT Decision Rights for Superior Results.* Harvard Business School Publishing.

8   National Audit Office (2008). *Managing Financial Resources to Deliver Better Public Services.*

9   Office of Government Commerce (2008). *Portfolio, Programme and Project Offices.* The Stationery Office, London.

10 HM Treasury. *The Green Book.* The Stationery Office, London.

11 Sanwal A. (2007). *Optimizing Corporate Portfolio Management.* Wiley.

Glossary

assurance

All the systematic actions necessary to provide confidence that the target (system, process, organization, programme, project, outcome, benefit, capability, product output, deliverable) is appropriate. Appropriateness might be defined subjectively or objectively in different circumstances. The implication is that assurance will have a level of independence from that which is being assured.

benefit

The measurable improvement resulting from an outcome perceived as an advantage by one or more stakeholders.

business as usual

The way the business normally achieves its objectives.

business change lifecycle

A generic name used to represent any organizational process or framework which helps to guide the delivery of programmes and projects using a collection of repeatable processes and decision points.

gated review

Structured reviews of a project, programme or portfolio as part of formal governance arrangements that are carried out at key decision points in the lifecycle to ensure that the decision to invest as per agreed business cases and plans remains valid.

governance

(Business change) Encompasses the structures, accountabilities and policies, standards and processes for decision-making within an organization in order for business change to answer the key strategic questions: 'Are we doing the right things?' 'Are we doing them the right way?' 'Are we getting them done well?' and 'Are we getting the benefits?'

groupthink

A term used to describe a group's style of thinking where the maintenance of the group's cohesion and togetherness becomes more important than the actual decision. Janis[4] defined it as 'a way of deliberating that group members use when their desire for unanimity overrides their motivation to assess all available plans of action.'

health check

A health check is a quality tool that provides a snapshot of the status of a project, programme or portfolio. The purpose of a health check is to gain an objective assessment of how well the project, programme or portfolio is performing relative to its objectives and any relevant processes or standards. A health check differs from a gated review in that it is a tool used for assurance purposes by the P3O to inform specific actions or capability maturity development plans, whereas a gated review is part of formal governance arrangements.

management board

Generic term used to describe project management boards, programme management boards, portfolio management boards or any combination of these based on the P3O context.

management dashboard
A technique to represent vast amounts of decision support information at an amalgamated level using tabular and graphical representation such as graphs and traffic lights.

organizational energy
Defined by the NHS Institute for Innovation and Improvement as 'the extent to which an organization has mobilized the full available effort of its people in pursuit of its goals'.

P3M3
The portfolio, programme and project management maturity model that provides a framework with which organizations can assess their current performance and put in place improvement plans.

portfolio
The totality of an organization's investment (or segment thereof) in the changes required to achieve its strategic objectives.

portfolio definition cycle
One of two continuous cycles within the portfolio management model containing portfolio management practices related to defining a portfolio.

portfolio delivery cycle
One of two continuous cycles within the portfolio management model containing portfolio management practices related to delivering a portfolio.

portfolio management
A co-ordinated collection of strategic processes and decisions that together enable the most effective balance of organizational change and business as usual.

portfolio office

An office which is established centrally to manage the investment process, strategic alignment, prioritization and selection, progress tracking and monitoring, optimization and benefits achieved by an organization's projects and programmes on behalf of its senior management.

Portfolio, Programme and Project Offices (P3O)

The decision-enabling and support business model for all business change within an organization. This will include single or multiple physical or virtual structures, i.e. offices (permanent and/or temporary), providing a mix of central and localized functions and services, and integration with governance arrangements and the wider business such as other corporate support functions.

PRINCE2™

A method that supports some selected aspects of project management. The acronym stands for PRojects IN Controlled Environments.

resource

An organization's physical or virtual entities (human or otherwise) that are of limited availability and can be used to undertake operations or business change.

senior responsible owner (SRO)

A UK government term for the individual responsible for ensuring that a project or programme of change meets its objectives and delivers the projected benefits. The person should be the owner of the overall business change that is being supported by the project.